I0414947

From Fear to Eternity:

A Path to Peace

Cassandra Curley

Also by Cassandra Curley

WHAT'S THE "MATTER"?:

The Key to Creating Your Reality

ಜಜಲ್ಲ

Dedicated to our beautiful daughters, Braden
Lorelle and Perrin Dure' - our Love personified.

ಜಜಣಣ

ISBN: 9781456378820

Contents

Part IV – Love...

Introduction: A Path to Peace

If we have no peace, it is because we have forgotten that we belong to each other. — **Mother Teresa**

To paraphrase Mother Teresa, when we have no Peace it is because we have forgotten that we are *part* of each other.

Indigenous cultures are inherently aware that it is our natural state to live harmoniously. But, as many unintentionally *choose* to live egocentrically, it disrupts the harmony. When we choose this path, it is most often because we have fallen for the belief in stories of separation.

When we dismiss, exclude, condemn, persecute or slaughter over contrasting beliefs, we *create* conflict. If so, what force causes us to ignore our innate impulse to unify, harmonize, and sustain life to commit such unnatural acts — what ignites this destructive force?

I believe all conflict is rooted in FEAR.

Born from an uncertainty about Life and strengthened with a forgetfulness of our intrinsic connection, Fear deprives Peace. Fear can only exist when there is uncertainty of Life's connectivity.

Our stories of separation emerged long ago within a paradise of innocent observations of the magnificence of Life and our connection to it. Naturally, these early perceptions of our world were attempts to understand our origin, relationships and relevance in the world. As we pondered our surroundings, we sensed an immutable connection to the Earth and knew we played an integral role in its abundance.

As time passed, we recognized cause and effect, noticed cycles and evolutions, and wondered about forces beyond our sight. We began to assign meaning to events that produced either pleasant or unfavorable outcomes. While seeking answers outside ourselves, we laid the foundation for judgment.

Eventually, our concepts of separation unleashed a self-centered impulse to fabricate distinctions through comparisons. "Us" and "ours" became "yours" and "mine". Paradoxically, this lens of division carried us further from our memories of unity. Ultimately, we even conjured hierarchies to label various levels of "themness" to reinforce our false stories of division.

In the end, the masses concluded that the world operates as countless parts, each uniquely suited for its purpose, yet virtually separate. **This longstanding belief of *exclusivity* is the myth that stole our Peace.** When we reduced the universe to a sum of its parts, we abandoned the truth that it began, emerged and functions as one.

With increased efforts to maintain our judgmental and fearful beliefs (after all, ideologies and dogma can be inextricably linked to our identities and loss of identity evokes fear), we stifled natural impulses to commune and we alienated fellow human beings. **This delusion of separation has allowed judgments to pervade, divisive concepts to endure and conflicts to perpetuate. As a consequence, we continue to witness extremes of disparity.**

Furthermore, institutions may take advantage of this delusion of division and sometimes *provoke* exclusionary practices to advance their own agendas. These conglomerates are not only destructive to the degree of insanity, but they can *reinforce* glaring inequity and endemic suffering.

Conversely, there is a burgeoning population of fearless human beings who have ignored the fallacy of separation and materialism, who recognize a widening chasm, and are seeking balance through unity. Amidst seemingly insurmountable differences, they understand the need to find a common ground and are willing to revolutionize the world for the sake of Humanity.

Languishing among these contrasting populations are most of our world's people – those who are perhaps, unaware, uninformed, complacent, apathetic or, oppressed. Together with intention, we can recreate a more cohesive world.

If truly desired, we could remember our original state of oneness, release the fear that creates the prevailing dichotomy and begin to live in Peace.

So, how can we cast out our divisive Fear of uncertainty about Life? How can we restore Peace? I believe we can be fearless by following Nature's example. Nature can show us a path to peace. After all, billions of years of evolutionary growth and abundance is evidence of its perfection. Devoid of Ego, Nature shows us how to grow effortlessly and without excess, adapt as necessary, seek harmony and balance, cultivate diversity and to protect only when growth is threatened. She provides the perfect model for equanimity. With her guidance, there is no reason to fear.

Fear is destructive, yet Nature is NEVER self-destructive. Yet, in just the last few centuries of the Industrial and Technological Revolutions, mankind has far exceeded an equitable balance of consumption and resources to disrupt its equilibrium and thwart its growth. The consequences of Mankind's actions to our planet and one another have been aberrant, destructive, and undeniable.

With Nature as our teacher, we can begin to remember that we are fundamentally the same and we can collectively draw upon our efforts and resources to THRIVE. We can rediscover our connection with one another and ignite the irrepressible power of synergy.

We have always been capable of Peace. Every one of the almost seven billion human beings on this planet desires it and was born with this natural understanding of oneness. We haven't lost it – it is inherent to our "being". We have simply forgotten.

There is hope.

Lightning strikes when opposite charges converge. For the sake of Humanity, we must neutralize a potentially explosive discharge before it is too late. In order to do so, we must undergo a revolutionary shift of thought and action by drawing upon the *inclusive* means that are shown in Nature. Her guidance is all we need

With willingness and commitment, we can create a tidal wave of change. Nothing is more powerful than the will to reserve differences and seek a common ground – it is the foundation of all transformations. At this crucial moment in time, we can transcend the notion of separation and concede that we *are* indeed a race of humans seeking "life, liberty and the pursuit of happiness". At this pivotal time in evolution, TRUTH can overshadow ignorance and willingness can overcome apathy. The outcome is ours to choose.

My hope is to inspire those who are seeking *transcendent* change to open their hearts and minds to global unity. As one of a family of twelve, I understand the power unity brings in its tendency for tolerance and cooperation – qualities often demonstrated in response to local, regional and global disasters, when our natural desire to connect and secure cooperative effort arises.

In an attempt to restore Peace, resistance is expected and understandable. After all, if it threatens to disrupt convention, it may activate that paralyzing FEAR of uncertainty, it may require concessions of living a LIE or, it may even provoke a fear of death. However, if traditional barriers are dismantled by Universal Truths, we can be fearless to experience the harmony demonstrated in Nature!

I intend to demonstrate that humanity can achieve personal and global accord if we open our minds and hearts to the Universal Truths reflected in Nature. Truth is self-evident, eternal and undeniable. With truth, we can abandon paradigms that usurp the Natural Order and shift *From Fear to Eternity.*

"Humanity is going to need a substantially new way of thinking if it is to survive!"   - **Albert Einstein**

How to Use This Book

*"When we try to pick out anything by itself, we find it hitched to everything else in the universe." - **John Muir***

This book is intended to provide a pathway to Peace. It is structured to present progressive, fundamental truths of Nature, to demonstrate that we are naturally peaceful and that conflict arises from fear.

Part I calls upon the reader to consider the universal connectivity of all Life, in that not only is there no separation, but every-thing effects the whole. Chapters 1 and 2 present the primary substance of Life and shows how the necessity of free will determines perspective. Chapters 3, 4 and 5 build to illustrate how every element of Nature has a unique structural frequency that resonates to effortlessly and harmoniously configure everything necessary for the Earth organism to THRIVE. Chapters 6 and 7 explain how similar frequencies entrain to increase amplitude and power, thus fortifying the expression of Life. The last chapter of Part I summarizes the preceding qualities of Life to reveal that Life itself is LOVE in physical form.

Part II shows how the virtual expression of Nature, being forever in the present moment of growth, has no use for Judgment

Part III explains how Judgment, absent from the Natural World, is founded in Fear.

Part IV concludes that the understanding of Life as eternal Love can release Fear and restore Peace.

PART I

All Life…

1

Is Conscious(ness)

"*There is no life without consciousness; there is no consciousness without life.*"

–Annie Besant

To understand how Nature models Peace, we must first bring awareness to "Universal Life". To do so, we must expand the thought of Nature beyond merely plants, animals (including humans) and their surroundings, and envision it as being all-encompassing and infinite. Consider Carl Sagan's view:

"*The cosmos are within us. We're made of star stuff. We are a way for the cosmos to know itself*".

His statement drew from the theory that an explosion of matter ignited Life – *all* substance has a common origin. With this foundation, we can begin to understand that our true essence has no divide, it has merely changed form.

Even more astounding is that the "stuff" we are made of has an immeasurable intelligence. The original "bang" and the subsequent transmutations were guided by an unseen force. Some type of awareness inspired change. Take a moment to embrace that thought:

All life is aware.

All life is… conscious(ness).

Although, it may seem daunting, allow me to guide you on a journey toward awareness. If you open your mind, you may "realize" what you perceive as "real" is rather a grand, optical illusion, in which *everything* is a part:

Beginning from your unique image of yourself, we can unravel the source of your being:

With the most basic understanding of the body, you may sense yourself as an entity in which all the different parts communicate – a constant input of information and reciprocating feedback. Now, in thought, travel to the level of awareness in which those parts communicate collectively as systems made of organs. In turn, those organs are made of tissue that responds in accordance with the information it receives. Then, imagine each cell of all the tissues as conscious sub-units interpreting and adjusting to every influx. Next, picture those cells' organelles (the nucleus and cytoplasm stuff) performing their inner and outer cellular functions with a united awareness. Further, imagine the compounds of each organelle sustaining its function while, the molecules of every compound play their suited role. Next, each element of every molecule resonate specific qualities. Hold the thought – we are almost there! Finally, visualize each element as atoms of protons, neutrons and electrons (essentially vibrating strings of attracted energy) that reduce to a unified field (Unifield) of energy. ***This*** **primordial essence *is* the life-force of reality *as* pure consciousness!**

The vision is incomplete so, please bear with me as we continue this journey from your unique vantage point of vibrating impulses (your body) outward – beyond everyone and everything in your household to all forms in your community. Now, expand that image to your city, state, country then, broader still to the continent – all connected by that same pulsating essence. Next, broaden that image to include the entire planet – from the epicenter of the core to all the planets in our solar system, to the billions of stars in our galaxy. It doesn't stop there - the Unifield continues to the <u>billions</u> of galaxies in the Universe - "to infinity and beyond" (a la Buzz Lightyear)! **Congratulations! You have just conceived of Universal Consciousness, the source from which all life arises.**

We have all undoubtedly heard Universal Consciousness termed by various other titles – God (or, the many alternate names for) by religious institutions, The Source, Life Energy or Life Force in Spiritual Circles; Zero Point Field (ZPF) by quantum scientists; Prana, Qi, Chi or Reiki in Eastern Philosophy; and Awareness, Thought or Pure Potentiality by New Thought Philosophers. Regardless of the name, it *is* the vital essence of life.

If you can grasp the vastness of our Unifield, the significance of each being may seem minute. If, on the other hand, you consider that reality is an ever-changing, adapting matrix, coalesced into individual forms within the whole, you will realize that every fluctuation is **connected**. Life is an intricate tapestry of inspired design!

One of our greatest challenges as **Humans Being** is to live in the awareness of the body while staying attuned to the unified whole – to "live *in* this world, not *of* it", as Jesus of Nazareth suggested.

"The conscious mind is a vehicle for the expression of the soul in corporeal terms."

- Jane Roberts, *The Nature of Personal Reality*, 1974

Conscious*ness* is our guide *and* facilitator. There are many unseen forces (sunshine, magnetism, gravity, electricity, and even *prayer*) that impact our lives. I am simply asking for a willingness to consider Universal Consciousness as the undercurrent from which all other energies flow.

ଞଓଗ

"The human consciousness is really homogenous. There is no complete forgetting, even in death." **- D. H. Lawrence**

ଞଓଗ

5

All Life…

Is Conscious(ness)

All Life...

2

Has Free Will

"The soul is crying for a reality experience which only physical life can give to it. The body is crying for an immortality experience, which only the soul can give it. As you permit the union to fulfill itself, you will directly know what it feels like to be the love that you are."

- Glenda Green, *Love Without End,* 1999

In Nature, free will is sacrosanct for growth.

Nature would never defy that which supports its growth – the choice is immutable. In fact, free will is perhaps, the preeminent edict of all Life. Religious traditions revere it, liberated political systems support it and Life would be meaningless without it. If not for free will, existence would merely be random discharges of biological impulses that carry no process for expansion.

However, unlike Nature, free will endows humanity with CHOICE and CHOICE IS THE ONLY MEANS FOR HUMANS TO **EXPERIENCE** LIFE! Free will integrates consciousness with physicality to allow every imaginable choice to generate accordant outcomes. In other words, every action has a reaction – it is up to us to decide.

Experience is necessary to create relativity (bodies come in handy for this). *As* consciousness in a physical form, we engage our corporeal selves to create experiences, evoke feelings in line with perceptions about any given choice, and establish a basis for comparison. As we build upon experiences, we formulate beliefs. All the while, free will governs the outcome as we hold the reigns over our choices.

Overall, our dual perspective of energetic and physical life makes perfect sense. If we were totally immersed in the physical world we could certainly have experiences but they would carry no meaning. The value of life comes in sensing the intrinsic purpose – to know who we are *contextually*, with all our glorious feelings and emotions! Otherwise, we would have no use for senses or, for that matter, a body at all. Urged by our Soul, choice grants the opportunity to discover who we are *capable* of being, while the body allows the means to interpret how we *feel* about each decision. This is why free will can never be denied.

All Life...

Is Conscious(ness)

Has Free Will

All Life...

3

Has a Unique Perspective

"You seem to be at the center of your world, because for you, your world begins with that point of intersection where soul and physical consciousness meet."

-Jane Roberts, *The Nature of Personal Reality*, 1974

Because we have free will to make choices, the unity of all things is perhaps the most difficult concept for us sensory-oriented humans to grasp. We ask, "How can we be a unique individual AND be a part of the whole?" While physical existence allows an endless opportunity for experiencing choices, it may impede our instinctive awareness of unity if the observer forgets reality is just a mirage.

As corporeal beings, we are inclined to perceive our surroundings as separate, tactile structures

– a predominately left-brain, linear function. Our interpretive brain derives its information from observing and storing sensory input. To concur, "things" are distinguished and labeled according to their looks, sound, scent, taste and/or feel. Structure provides differentiation as "symbolic game pieces" as we play "Life".

However, the right brain has a capacity to sense a more abstract quality of life. Among other things, this hemisphere enables us to express creativity, discern emotion and process the sense of connection to all things.

We know about this dual nature of perception and even describe ourselves as either "left-brained" or "right-brained". Furthermore, these contrasting qualities tend to express as masculine and feminine aspects of ourselves. Nevertheless, the duality of awareness challenges us to straddle between two seemingly separate worlds of physical and intuitive realities, while questioning how to function as living beings and stay attuned to all Life. To achieve this goal, we must use an expansive view.

Individual perceptions of separation (judgments, biases, prejudices) may be derived through experience and teachings, but by maintaining objectivity, that division fades. The 2004 movie *Crash* depicts this concept superbly. The storyline connects several racially-charged events to demonstrate how each incident can domino to impact several lives. In turn, each person is given an opportunity to perceive their views from a different perspective, thereby, producing more tolerance. As an outside observer of the film, we are allowed an objective view of how perspectives can alter realities.

Even though uniqueness is a hallmark of life forms, separation is not. Only the human Ego (the self-image) sees form as separate. In truth, all living things are individuations of the same fundamental energy source configured in such a way as to *appear* different. Much like the way individual photographs can be positioned to create an illusion of a larger whole, individual forms have arisen to create a diverse and biodynamic Earth.

The concept of a uni-verse is codified in my previous book by explaining that **all tangible existence arises from and is unified by an energy source that conforms to the belief behind thought, word and action.** You are part of that energy source, it is part of you, and you cannot remove yourself from it. In other words, **all of life arises from the same**

fundamental source and physical reality is created by your belief! This statement is the most pervasive and imperative concept in this text so, let me reemphasize:

BASED ON YOUR DISTINCT PERSPECTIVE, ALL LIFE IS WHAT YOU BELIEVE IT TO BE.

As demonstrated by Quantum Physics and concurring with ancient wisdom, reality is merely a clever illusion. In actuality, there is no division between one thing and another. The physical forms we see comprise only about 1% of the universe and that portion is more than 99% vibrating energy that is stabilized in such a way as to seem solid - there is no "beginning" or "end".

"Matter is bound up energy and energy is liberated matter."
John Keely, 1883

Nevertheless, while the *distinctiveness* (the localized image) of this universal energy reflects the brilliant complexity of life, it may mistakenly be perceived as separation. Since everything and everyone is differentiated by its own unique formation of energy, objects *appear* individualized and comparisons often ensue. As part of this collective delusion, we have assigned forms as "this" or "that" and location as "here" opposed to "there". It enables us to conduct our physical lives.

"For as he thinketh in his heart, so is he." - **Proverbs 23:7, King James Version**

However, by considering our oneness, we can see ourselves as an extension of everything and more readily value the immediate effect each of our actions has upon all life. If our life source *is* primary and universal, then any thought, word or action *must* transmit without interference.

Although relativity serves a useful purpose by providing a context in which to structure the environment, it may create judgment when the **mind** takes the apparent for the absolute. Let me offer an example: You would say it is nighttime if it were dark outside, although, a view from space would clearly show that night on Earth is simply a different perspective in relation to the Sun, not an opposite of day.

On occasion, my mother would playfully mimic my Paternal Grandmother by saying, "That's just the way they are, Johnnie." Grandma Terry's view on the unique nature and temperament of individuals had been shared with my father (John), who in turn, expressed the sentiment wisely to my family as, "It's all relative." That is, everything depends on your point of view. They were both stating that individual perception in our Earthly existence is subjective – we each conceive life through our own filter of experiences and choices to create a unique perspective.

Cultural and economic perspectives can lead to comparable distinctions. For instance, some may afford a privileged upbringing and see the world as abundant and luxurious, while others may have faced hardship and therefore, experience life as a struggle. Others, who live communally or off the land, may experience life as cooperative and equitable, while, entire populations may harbor hatred built on the view of separation and judgment. As long as any perspective remains confined to a localized point of view, there will be no other reality.

Have you ever wondered why certain people remain in circumstances that seem unbearable? It is likely that they have not been exposed to other views. Remember, most of the almost seven billion human beings on Earth have had limited access to books, much less, a television or the internet. How can they conceptualize "more", "plenty" or "freedom" if they have no basis for comparison? Of course, the reverse is also true: "You never know how good you have it until…" Therefore, relationships provide the opportunity for context.

From the sublime to the radically brutal, there are as many different perspectives as there are individuals – each in alliance with experience and conforming to the observer.

In Psychology, it is well-known that infants perceive their bonded caretakers as part of their self – they do not discern a separation. Perhaps, this is their untainted awareness of being one the world.

As we develop, we are systematically taught about "things" ("a stove is hot", "this is a doggie", "that is bad"), we gain experiences for context, and most often, unlearn our oneness.

Experience may create a diverse palette from which to make choices but it also develops a greater challenge to maintain our awareness of unity. However, if allowed a broad enough viewpoint, the impression of separation blurs. To clarify, imagine the view of Earth from outer space again. In this vision, there is no here or there – it is a living planet. There is no them or us – it is a world of people. There is no

17

right way or wrong way – merely, different ways. If the view remains expansive, even happiness and suffering can be seen as relative.

To repeat, it is easy to fall for the illusion of separation if your perspective is limited. However, by remembering that we are each a local reflection of a universal source and understanding perspectives are derived from experience, we can willfully generate awareness capable of changing the world. Awakening to the image of a holistic, consciously created life *is* transformational – it signifies the beginning of the end to self-righteousness, superiority and delusions of separation. This concept, renewed in the hearts of as many receptive souls as possible, will be revolutionary.

The solution is to maintain an awareness of both. Therein casts a meaning within the statement, "being in this world, not of it."

Unlike our innate perspective of unity, the illusion of separation is an affliction of the Ego. Our Soul knows only unified bliss, while the Ego believes it is purely physical and will tenaciously fight to satisfy its material desires through the senses. Therefore, when we live in a world in which we seek fulfillment through external means alone, the effect is temporary. Addiction is an extreme example of this misdirected effort to achieve bliss. To paraphrase an olden sage, "substances are the **Ego's** attempt at ecstasy." The Ego falsely believes that we *are* our body while the soul knows we *use* a body.

So, why is it that we *need* a body – why are we here on earth living this dichotomy of life? If, the immortal, eternal soul has always been blissful, how could it possibly KNOW any other state, unless there was a basis for comparison? Therefore, **Life provides the opportunity to create unique perspectives through relative experience. It allows us to implement what we know we know (with spirit) with what we think we know (with the mind).** As such, the arrangement provides an ideal environment – we can "sense" and interpret our surroundings in context rather than just conceptually (your parents may have *warned* you not to drink too much alcohol, but you had to *experience* it to really understand why). Plainly, this is how we qualify our mortal existence.

Whereas, the soul knows only oneness, the linear mind may take structure too seriously and forget that we are all just in the process of co-creating. "I am here, you are there, we are all autonomous" is what the structured mind believes. If it **dominates**, it obscures our higher sense of unity consciousness. **Rather than**

viewing all things as interdependent parts of the whole, it can perceive separation and cast judgment.

When you observe someone, are you inclined to see them simply as a sacred fellow being or do you instantly label them as maybe, "overweight" or "underdressed"? Have you ever pegged someone as "foreign" by their features or garb? These comparisons are dependent on context and a perception of differences. Notice how those perceptions can change within a different context: The master painter, Peter Paul Reubens, was reknowned for his "fleshy" female nudes and in the 1920s, a woman with extra weight was considered "voluptuous" and proportionate; on many European beaches, sunbathers go topless without thought of impropriety; and, in the diversely populated New York City there are so many ethnic residents that differences are hardly noticeable after time.

Most people *learn* to compare and contrast – leading our dual awareness of structure and unity to bring about conflicting thoughts. However, if viewed *through* the lens of UNITY, we can picture physical life holistically – there would be no comparison. "The eyes are a window to (and from) the soul" then makes perfect sense. Within this vision comes the erosion of the illusion of separation and *an end to Judgment!* **JUDGMENT CAN ONLY EXIST IF ONE THING IS COMPARED TO ANOTHER.**

Ultimately, Life *is* what we collectively believe it to be. The divine paradox of life is it only becomes "real" or "physical" if we believe it to be, even as, all physicality is an illusion, predicated by belief.

Therefore, if each vantage point affords its unique perspective, how could anything be "incorrect" within the framework of the individual? It is simply a culmination of the belief behind experiences, as every experience provides an opportunity to decide how to feel about it. This is a very powerful statement – **every belief is based on a point of view.** If any aspect does not resonate, **we hold the power of free will to change it.**

"You are responsible for your own thoughts – once you realize that your thoughts form reality, then, you are no longer a slave to events."
-Jane Roberts, *The Eternal Validity of the Soul*, 1972

All Life…

Is Conscious(ness)

Has Free Will

Has a Unique Perspective

All Life...

4

Is Effortless

"Consider the lilies of the field, how they grow; they toil not, neither do they spin. And yet I say unto you, that even Solomon in all his glory was not arrayed like one of these."

- Matthew 6:28-29

Nature is unfalteringly efficient – even as it holds no perception of an energy shortage, it still expends only enough energy to achieve growth – while leaving no waste. Rather, its "perceived waste" is an effortless contribution toward the continuous cycle of Life. Per Physics, this follows *The Law of Conservation of Energy* or more commonly, *the path of least resistance*. **As it is intrinsically conscious and interconnected, Nature persists effortlessly**. A more meaningful interpretation of this concept could be that *Nature*

23

follows the most efficient means of expressing growth. Growth is Life – expressed.

In the Natural world, the path of least resistance is always taken by objects moving through a system (water running down a mountainside is a prime example). There are many other ways Nature demonstrates this economy of energy. For instance, lightning flowing through a circuit behaves similarly. While every available path has some current moving through it, the amount of current through each path is inversely proportional to its electrical resistance. Even atmospheric disturbances (storms) flow on the path of least resistance by flowing toward zones of low barometric pressure where lower air density offers less impedance to the storm system than higher pressure zones. An ultimate example of Life's efficiency is expressed through a single fertilized egg or germinated seed – Life sparked and emergent.

"In every seed is the promise of thousands of forests."
Deepak Chopra, MD, Spiritual Luminary

When hearing Dr. Chopra make the previous statement, it brought a sense of wonder by imagining expansive woodlands increasing to the breadth of a continent – all from a single acorn. You need only note the Amazon Rain Forest to see Nature does not resist expansion. When left unimpeded, how awesome her efficiency can be.

It is the Human Ego that sees Life as separate and impedes *our* growth. We possess the means to achieve even our most basic needs and desires by tapping into the Unifield of infinite energy with conscious intent (after all, it *is* an *unlimited source of creation*). Yet, we allow the illusion of separation to sabotage us again and again. We let our preconceived notions create unwarranted obstacles. The illusions of "can't" or "lacking" impairs our connection to instant manifestation because we have obscured ourselves from the truth.

Manifesting effortlessly is not a concept held exclusively for Nature, as we are a part of Nature! The Nike slogan *"Just do it!"* is more than just a catchy phrase, it is a message for Humanity. The only thing that prevents us from achieving any particular outcome is the limitation of our beliefs. What goal has ever been attained by someone believing "I can't do that"? Do you think that Michael Phelps told himself that, "If I'm lucky, I may win eight Olympic gold medals in swimming" or that the unparalleled success that Oprah Winfrey, a black woman with a challenging childhood, has achieved in business was unintentional? Only the belief that life *has* to be a struggle sustains that arduous reality – it is a fabrication of the mind.

All Life…

Is Conscious(ness)

Has Free Will

Has a Unique Perspective

Is Effortless

"Nature does not hurry, yet everything is accomplished."
Lao Tzu, Founder of Taoism

All Life...

5

Seeks Harmony

Har-mo-ny *n.* Agreement in feeling, approach, action, disposition or the like; sympathy; **accord.**

American Heritage Dictionary, 1969

Earthly life accounts for the most abundant biosphere in our galaxy. Moreover, our planet, like the Human Body, is a self-sustaining entity. Put in simpler terms, Earth is a gigantic, living organism. And, like bacteria are to our bodies, we are "bacteria" to the Earth! To conceive this concept, visualize the earth as analogous to a human body:

Similar to our complementary and diverse body systems (Skeletal, Muscular, Circulatory, etc.)

seeking balance, the Earth's systems seek stability, or homeostasis. The tectonic plates protectively encrust the planet's surface like a huge exoskeleton moving languidly by its molten muscles beneath; massive water systems circulate life-sustaining fluid, while aiding in regulating temperature and creating a barrier "skin"; flowing air assists water and acts as a superficial lymphatic system to compel particles on land, sea and air, depositing them strategically; plants, as part of the enormous respiratory system, "inhale" carbon dioxide, absorb sunlight, water and nutrients for survival and then, "exhale" life-giving oxygen in return. Additionally, they provide food in a digestive cycle of nutrients; even lightning, like synaptic messages from our brain, can compare to deliberate electrical impulses broadcast across the lands; all the while, Humans and animals colonize as TRILLIONS UPON TRILLIONS of "probiotics" that function interdependently in the continuous cycle of life. This diverse, but unified, image of Mother Earth as a giant, living organism is crucial to understanding the synergy that sustains a universal being.

For billions of years, our planetary body has flawlessly supported life with instinctive checks and balances. In synch with influences of its environment (often Mankind), it responds **holistically** to maintain equilibrium. From the lightest touch (the "Butterfly Effect"), to major disturbances, our planet adapts to restore balance: an earthquake deep in the depths of the Pacific Ocean will respond with tsunamis, floods, wind changes and the like before readjusting; in the aftermath of a meteoric collision, our celestial host eventually recovered from The Ice Age; after being barraged with nuclear explosions, Nagasaki and Hiroshima are again habitable; even as you read, the Earth is fending off an onslaught of billions of tons of man-made waste and emissions; and tragically, as I type these words, it is enduring an monumental assault as a cut in the ocean's floor is bleeding millions of gallons of oil. When the wound eventually heals, adjustments will begin to occur. What changes will offset this unnatural incident? We will soon find out.

As the Earth seeks harmony at a macroscopic level, so our body, our systems, our tissue and our cells do microscopically. There is no part of our person that is not aware of the whole and no part of the whole that is not aware of the parts. Even as we may flush and get goose bumps when hearing an inspirational story, or feel grief and sorrow with our entire being at the loss of a loved one, every cell experiences the emotion.

Likewise, an urgent event (like a broken bone) would call the entire body into action – EVERY CELL IN THE BODY WOULD BE AWARE! First, you would feel PAIN (your body's alarm system) to alert you of the damage. Next, the body's nervous system would engage to direct blood, oxygen and nutrients while, osteoblasts replicate and mobilize for repair. There is nothing that the physical body does not sense in its function to support itself and it does not stop at the level of the cells.

Envision each cell as a conscious sub-unit that constantly interprets its external environment via millions of receptor sites in the cell membrane. Accordingly, they consciously control the response to, and passage of, all substances necessary for survival.

Now, what force implements these impulses?

All Life…

Is Conscious

Has Free Will

Has a Unique Perspective

Is Effortless

Seeks Harmony

All Life...

6

Attracts

"Do you know what one mirror said to the other mirror?"

No.

"It's all done with people."

- Neale Donald Walsch, *The New Revelations, 2002*

If it has been established that the totality of Life arises from consciousness, that we are endowed with free will to make choices and evoke feelings about the consequences; that awareness and feedback creates a unique perspective, and that Life is meant to flow effortlessly in harmony, then what compels the coalescence of physical reality? The answer can be found within the pervasive concept called the Law of Attraction.

Understanding the mechanisms of physical reality is no easy task. It is not my intention, nor my desire, to produce a book of Quantum Physics, Newtonian Physics, Chemistry, Biology, or especially, start a philosophical debate about the subject. There are endless volumes of work to support the forthcoming statements and I have been careful to include only the most relevant and necessary elements. With that in mind, I will attempt to integrate all of the above and present the Law of Attraction most simply as:

LIKE ATTRACTS LIKE

All of life must abide by sovereign Laws of Reality and the most basic is that **all physical form obeys consciousness – it attracts what is perceived.** Consciousness is the incipient power that directs all structure, and perception is the glue that binds it. In other words, CONSCIOUSNESS IS THE ATTRACTOR FIELD THAT SYNCHRONIZES PERCEPTION WITH MANIFESTATION.

To go further, consciousness is the Unifield of unlimited possibilities that effortlessly attracts and solidifies belief. In Quantum Physics, the unlimited potential of consciousness is called the Zero Point Field (the point of perfect equilibrium and simultaneity). In New Thought, it is called The Now; in Eastern Philosophy, it is called Being in the Moment.

As such, **Nature is pure consciousness in physical form. It is sentient energy that exists in the perpetual present with a sole intention to GROW.** This is why Nature provides a perfect model for equanimity. If we need proof of effortless harmony, we have Nature, unencumbered by Fear or Doubt, to demonstrate.

As beliefs are sustained through consciousness, thought is the activator that invokes a change in vibration to attract the conjured image. The more persistently and collectively the thoughts are projected, the more reinforced and amplified the reality becomes. Like a chorus of voices singing the same song, our physical reality is a literal reflection of our shared tunes.

Forgive the redundancy but, the importance of this concept cannot be overstated, yet it is difficult for many to grasp. To reiterate in simple terms: **The nature of reality is that you attract what you believe in direct proportion to your belief.** When amplified with similar (or group) beliefs, attraction strengthens the reality.

As consciousness underlies the appearance of physical matter, it can be understood through Laws of Quantum Physics, but as matter is perceived with our five senses, the Laws of Newtonian Physics apply. This dichotomy of views creates havoc between the "I've got to see it to believe it" (a predominate view) and the "I've got to believe it to see it" adherents.

If this concept is still difficult to grasp, think of it this way: On the television series Star Trek: The Next Generation, the crew often experienced dual realities on the Holodeck. This was a level of the ship in which participants, through the technology of holograms, could create almost any reality they chose. It was all smoke and mirrors but, they became immersed in the illusion. Life on Earth is very much the same. Our temporal lives are like a virtual reality game we participate in to exert our free will and gain experience. Perception attracts (creates) the reality.

To emphasize the extent of the power of Belief, consider that similar thought waves congregate (attract) and amplify to strengthen each other. The stronger the thoughts become, the greater the reality prevails. Most importantly is recognizing how this applies to biases, fears, phobias, and habits – all are transfixed thoughts in the mind.

To take respective beliefs one step further, it is easy to see how formidable group beliefs can attract with enough intensity as to create polarized systems. The stronger the contrasting systems, the greater the polarity becomes. Adamant views of "My Way" versus "Your Way" have created excessive fear and conflict in the world. That is, unique life perspectives have created different perceptions, which have resulted in different realities.

Ironically, in today's volatile atmosphere of fear, the primary obstacle of those calling for change is fear of change.

"...the only thing we have to fear is fear itself – nameless, unreasoning, unjustified terror which paralyzes needed efforts to convert retreat into advance." – FDR

Ultimately, Beliefs transform thought into matter by transmuting impulses throughout the Unifield, by altering the elemental structure of molecules, by activating latent DNA. and by directing the Unifield to affect cellular function. Cellular Biologist, Bruce Lipton explains these mechanisms brilliantly in his book, The Biology of Belief and the expanded audio version, The Wisdom of Your Cells".

If we understand that the Central Nervous and Enteric (gut) Systems provide *local* interpretation and storage of sensory experiences, whereas, the soul (our unique imprint of consciousness) supplies the essential vitality, we can see that we are not our bodies, but a reflection of the totality of our beliefs.

Imagine the global shift that could occur if a mass of humanity were to view the world as an extension of itself!

Presently, highly polarized beliefs could culminate in a volatile release. Again, like lightning in a thunderstorm, the discharge is Nature's method of equilibrium. At any point in history, we can choose to neutralize polarities with unity or, we can strike with fearful conflict. May our resolution be PEACE.

All Life...

Is Conscious

Has Free Will

Has a Unique Perspective

Is Effortless

Seeks Harmony

Attracts

All Life...

7

Expresses Life

"If you do not go within, you go without."

Neale Donald Walsch, *Conversations with God*

Life *expresses* life. Yet, science does not offer sufficient evidence as to how and why life exists. Scientists can calculate with certainty that life perpetuates, that it is indeed animated and that it generates in predictable patterns but, until a fundamental substance, the so-called "God Particle", is isolated and explored, science is not collectively willing to accept the *source* of life as anything other than tangible. Accordingly, Life *remains* Science's biggest mystery.

On the other hand, **humans being** question meaning in Life. We may accept that we are biological beings, capable of reasoning and born with an instinct for survival but, we are equally imbued with a desire to share love, be creative, show compassion and find purpose – qualities that are beyond measure. To deny that we possess these traits would betray their very existence, so we appease ourselves by conjuring up some unseen power that may provide their source. If we see all things as separate, we surmise the force could only be outside ourselves. However, if we retain the dualistic view of life as a physical apparition <u>and</u> collective consciousness, we can "real-ize" ourselves as spiritual beings within physical bodies. Let me attempt to clarify:

Some people may believe that their genes are the master controller and everything is predetermined – like the hard drive of a computer. This notion is incomplete. Others may feel that the brain controls the entire body, much like a computer's operating system. That idea is also lacking. **In truth, consciousness, like an endless supply of electrical current (to keep the computer analogy), is the *primary* source that guides our physical body.**

Incredible as it seems, cells obey as the mind *interprets*. Thought influences the DNA to switch on and off segments of their chains to either activate or suppress codes (the field of Epigenetics explores this phenomenon). As a result, our body constantly conforms to the information our *beliefs* broadcast. Therefore, our current condition is an **image-ination in-formation** of the Mind/Body and Spirit (i.e. Brain/Genetic Blueprint and Consciousness). Every time you are "sick with worry", "elated with happiness" or "full of anger", your body responds with a cascade of corresponding hormones, peptides and neurotransmitters (the chemical equivalents of thought) to create physiological changes. These changes are not fleeting – they actually begin to reprogram cells to adapt to the input. The cells will store this new information until they perceive otherwise.

When you view life as a reflection of Mind/Body and Spirit, your state of being becomes more clear: the **Brain** interprets the **Past** experiences from stored memory to provide the DNA blueprint for the **Present Body** to obey and the interwoven **Spiritual Consciousness** guides you to the promise of a **Future reunited in Oneness.**

Likewise, when groups of like-minded individuals create dynamic realities, it is sustained in accordance with their beliefs. Just as thoughts affect the human body, collective thoughts affect the human race.

Whereas, Life expressing Life through Life *drives* all Life, Nature remains present to its influx of information. It does not reflect or project false perceptions, but rightly receives information and "presents" the most viable aspect of itself. In this way, Nature creates diversity and synergy to reinforce itself.

"Once something grows, it seeks the highest form of itself – the best star, dinosaur, fern, or amoeba. When that form is exhausted, it makes a transition to a new form that is more creative and interesting."

- Deepak Chopra, *Reinventing the Body, Resurrecting the Soul*, 2009

All Life…

Is Conscious

Has Free Will

Has a Unique Perspective

Is Effortless

Seeks Harmony

Attracts

Expresses Life

All Life...

8

Is Love

"Love is a canvas furnished by Nature and embroidered by imagination."

- Voltaire

Throughout this book, a forgotten truth has been alluded to but not revealed. In fact, it is not really forgotten, it has merely been overshadowed by fear, for it resides eternally in our hearts as certainly as life itself. It is a truth so powerful, a power so truthful, that it would change the world in an instant if it were fully realized. Still, fear has cast a spell of forgetfulness on humanity that can only be broken with a willingness to set aside all delusions of separation and express the true power of **Love.**

Love is forever revered, idealized, romanticized and commercialized for agreeably, it is the greatest power Mankind is capable of wielding. It so encompasses our being that we endlessly long to experience it, would not hesitate to die for it and would perish without it. However, in the world of structure, Love may be misconceived as something we long to attain rather than a source in and of itself. The magnitude of its power will remain unleashed until we truly understand the revelation that… *we are Love.* It is not something outside our self, like a commodity to be bought or sold. Love *is* the essence of all Life. It is synonymous with Universal Consciousness, Awareness, The Zero Point Field, Life Force, the Attractor Field (power of attraction), the Unifield or, if God is Love and we are made in the image of God, also **God** *Personified.*

Like a junkie seeking his or her next fix, it is no wonder we crave the experience of love – our bodies are built to thrive with its awareness. An act of kindness toward a stranger, a parent's loving embrace, serving the needs of another who is in desperation or pain, risking ones life for the benefit of others are all aspects of being who we truly are. Being Love brings contentment like no other condition because it is our genuine state of being. There is a true chemical and spiritual feeling of goodness that exudes and nourishes us, which nothing synthetic can substitute. Our bodies literally change in composition and vibrate at a different frequency when we act as an extension of love.

However, when Love has been misconstrued, maligned and falsified to satisfy the desires of the Ego, Fear finds a home. Fear activates obsession over control, and control only exists in the world of structure. That is, it is fooled by the illusion of separation and limitations, rather than the truth of unlimited potential.

Fear is the source of all conflict because it judges and condemns, whereas, Love is the solvent that disperses all fear, because it unites and accepts. Fear can only thrive when we detach ourselves from knowing our true self *as absolute and eternal Love*. Otherwise, what would we have to fear? Death? Death of what?

Love holds dominion over all reality by commanding all of reality for, nothing supersedes the power of love. Many enlightened beings have demonstrated this truth with acts that have transcended the world of structure to create what could be called miracles.

There is no limit to the power of love and our ability to harness its potential, save the limit of our belief about it. However, any attempt to quantify it in an equation, isolate it as a particle, or capture its essence in a formula has remained elusive because, it has been pursued through the world of structure. Only Nature, through a perfect model, expresses Love's existence.

"There are only two ways to live your life. One is as though nothing is a miracle, the other is as though everything is a miracle."

- Albert Einstein

All Life...

Is Conscious

Has Free Will

Has a Unique Perspective

Is Effortless

Seeks Harmony

Attracts

Expresses Life

Is Love

Part II

Nature…

9

Is MANifest Consciousness

"The world is only the physical aspect of God."

– Paul Coelho, *The Alchemist*, 1988

To help visualize a global picture of Nature's mastery, go back to the image of our planet as a macrocosm of a single, pulsating life form. Fuse that with our original concept of universal consciousness and you may be able to picture our world as the *physical form* of Earthly Consciousness. If our bodies are the MANifested reflection of *our* total awareness and all life is connected, we must all be co-creating (a

"Collective Consciousness" as Carl Jung called it)! To put this in the same language as earlier, Earth *is* manifest consciousness. As such, the Earth and its inhabitants *represent* our collective conscience – the origin of which, in its purest physical form, was sun and water.

Until recently, qualities of sun and water have been a mystery. How can light act as both particle and wave energy and why does water seem to harmonize with its environment? Both queries can be answered with "They are part of consciousness, just as we are".

To "shed more light" on light, the twentieth century, renowned physicists, Hendrik Lorentz, Henri Poincaré, Albert Einstein, Niels Bohr and David Bohm, among others, showed that light behaves as a particle or a wave based on the observer. If the observer expects the substance to act as infinitesimal pellets, they do. Likewise, if the observer believes that light influences as a radiant wave, the same is true. It conforms to whichever belief predominates – the same way our beliefs effect reality. Whole libraries of books and millions of entries on the internet expound the wonders of sunshine and the mysteries of water.

Although it covers more than seventy percent of the Earth's surface, and accounts for about as much of our make-up, water is a scientific enigma. It has unique properties and qualities unlike any other substance. Water is the only compound found naturally in all four states of matter (liquid, gaseous, solid and plasma), which enables its continuous cycle from bodies of water to condensed clouds (100% humidity, yet suspended in air?) and frozen ice-caps, back to precipitation and run-off, returning into bodies of water; it has a high specific heat index allowing it to absorb a lot of heat before it changes temperature; it has a high surface tension which causes clumping and accounts for its droplet formations and capillary action; it is called the universal solvent as it dissolves and transports vital nutrients and matter; as a solid, its structure forms into hexagonal shapes that provide immense stability while creating less dense mass - which is why ice floats.

With their ubiquitous presence and immense connection with life-force, the marriage of water and sunlight provides the fundamental medium for **Life to express itself.** We know that the sun provides power for plants through photosynthesis and that the stored energy that that process creates and, ultimately releases through assimilation, is essential for all life. Of course, radiant energy also provides the added benefits of thermal heat and acts as a catalyst for many metabolic functions in life – serving much like an amplifier of vitality. We also agree that water, with its exceptional qualities, is necessary to sustain all living things but, are you aware that SUN + WATER = LIFE? Science has finally shown that **sufficient sunshine and water are indeed, the Earth's primary physical equivalents of consciousness!**

This concept has been theorized for many years but was customarily shunned by the scientific community due to lack of "evidence". However, in the last few years, the integration of Newtonian and Quantum Physics has demonstrated what spiritual teachers have shared for centuries – *in the presence of sufficient sunlight, water begets Life.* It is no wonder that in Biblical times, the world was said to have begun with light and water and that water was the symbol for attraction!

To help validate these claims are studies conducted by Dr. Gerald Pollack, Professor and researcher at the University of Washington, in his book, *Cells, Gels and the Engines of Life,* and Masaru Emoto, researcher and author (two of many pioneers in the quest to answer questions about these miraculous substances). After decades of research, Pollack has shown that, in the presence of light, water ionizes (mobilizes electrons) to create a polarization and generate a micro-current. As long as light permeates water, a strengthening polarization occurs to form more of a plasma gel quality. The more prolonged the sunlight, the greater the collection of growth. He theorizes that the creation of this electrical impulse was the original spark of life – the genesis of which all life emerged. Emoto has taken more radical, yet convincing, approach in demonstrating water's harmony to consciousness. He has captured images of the effects of intention on the crystallization of water. Under controlled conditions, the studies repeatedly show that when positive thoughts are bestowed upon samples of water, it forms beautiful, symmetric formations and when negative thoughts are projected, the formations are chaotic and disfigured. The Sun as a perpetual generator, and water as the most abundant substance, ascend from the matrix of Life as expressions of Life.

Nature...

10

Does Not Judge

"Never does nature say one thing and wisdom another."

- Juvenal, *Satires*

Nature does not think – she simply *is* **Love in action.** She expresses life effortlessly, through the same universal laws humans are subject to, without an Ego to interfere. She is not deterred by a belief in structure, therefore, **she does not judge,** and is able to access the unlimited potential for creation. In kind, she avails us with an ideal environment to sustain and experience life, and is a divine model for peace and equanimity.

Unlike Humans, Nature continuously models adaptability and sustainability by seeking life efficiently and in harmony through unfettered consciousness. Even after a cataclysm, like the Ice Age, she gives no *thought* to survival. Nature does not consider whether there is enough to go around, she does not resist regeneration, she simply continues anew. Like the seasons and cycles of life, Nature's majesty is replenishing, perpetual and abundant.

In comparison, we can see how thoughts of separation and structure misguide us (i.e., "there is not enough", "every man for himself", "yours is the wrong way" or "profitability takes precedent") and result in a self-imposed cycle of destruction and stagnation, followed by retrospect and ultimately, renewal. This pattern has repeated throughout history.

"In society, structure is most protected by those who have attained what they want and, ironically, those who have so little that any thoughts of more loss are simply unbearable. They also blindly obey it. This is the harmony between the rich and the poor. By contrast, those who establish and implement values based on moderation and mobility use enough structure to make life work without inhibiting growth or freedom."

-Glenda Green, *Jesus Speaks: Love Without End*

After the Persian Wars, The Golden Age of Greece lasted until wars with Sparta crushed their civilization; the lavish Roman Empire collapsed after over-expansion and the invasion of Germanic Tribes; following centuries of a "Dark Age", powered by a reign of suppression and intolerance, The Renaissance (literally, "rebirth") brought forth a revival of beauty in art and culture; the Age of Enlightenment celebrated the potential of the human spirit until the time the Napoleonic Wars ended it in death and destruction; our own Declaration of Independence in the *United* States was soon marred by conflicting beliefs fought out in the Civil War; presently, there is constant bickering about ideologies that has created chasms in the human race. When we judge and allow beliefs in separation to command, we suppress our true nature of Love:

"It is the mark of true civilization to manage both phases of expansion and compression with equal grace...this is reality. However, it is the mark of structure and illusion to generate the misconception that expansion is the only route to power and glory. When a nation or society has centered its power primarily on structure and illusion, it will be driven compulsively to continue expansion at all costs... The great misconception is that with enough force and manipulation, any idea can be made to work. That is the God [Love] separated concept."

Glenda Green, *Jesus Speaks: Love Without End*, 1999

At this stage of our evolution, we do not have to allow our Egos to lead us on a path of self-destruction. With a change of thought, we can finally enable means to coexist in a peaceful manner.

It seems as though humans go through these cycles intentionally – maybe creating disunity for the very purpose of illuminating unity (as I have written throughout this book, relativity is our only way of processing physical reality). As such, conflict does put life in perspective and often brings a new appreciation for simple pleasures. Conflict can even shine the light on ultimate TRUE MIGHT by providing us with the opportunity to show love to our supposed enemies. However, when we acknowledge the truth that we are indeed, connected in spirit to everything *as Love*, there is no need to experience conflict. Rather, we can alter our errant ways and see that every being is an extension of our self.

"Your entrapment in this cycle of violence has been an a-maze-ment, and your release from this cycle of violence will be achieved by your at-one-ment — or what you would call atONEment."

-Neale Donald Walsch, *The New Revelations*, 2002

An *Age of Peace* is being thwarted by Fear and the stubborn resistance to the simple truth of Unity. Ironically, if we would just **choose** to follow Nature's example of unanimity, harmony and abundance would prevail.

If all Life…

is conscious,

has free will,

has a unique perspective,

is effortless,

seeks harmony,

attracts,

expresses life,

and is Love,

and Nature, the perfect model, does not judge then, only…

JUDGMENT CREATES CONFLICT!

Part III

Judgment...

11

Is Founded in Fear

"The ultimate outcome in life is never in doubt. Doubt has created fear. If you doubt outcome, you doubt God [Love]. If you doubt God, you must live in fear and guilt."

Neale Donald Walsch, *Conversations With God, 1998*

Judgment is founded in fear because our Ego has let it blind our vision of oneness, and deceived us into believing we are powerless. The Ego is very adept at deception and mocking Love. As mankind has allowed, *actually facilitated*, Fear's stronghold in the media, politics, relationships and much of our spiritual beliefs, we have relegated Love to a level of idealism, rather than its rightful place of power. We have let ourselves be fooled into believing we are *not* omnipotent Love.

As a result, many institutions (to maintain their own survival) prey on our fears as though we have no mind of our own, and we play into it as though we have no volition of our own.

Of course, when we are constantly barraged with images of separation and judgment, it becomes increasingly difficult to maintain a sense of unity. But, if we would just *listen* to our heart and gauge our perceptions through the filter of Love, fear would be eliminated, because we would *know* that we are our *own* source of power and that anything else is an illusion – we would have nothing *to* fear.

Likewise, if we were to discern with Love, we would cast no judgment, for we would know that every being is acting from their own perspective and would treat them accordingly.

In turn, if we were to take action *through* Love, it would dissolve any differences because Love has no polarity (since it is the essence of all reality, it acts as a universal solvent). Think about any time you may have

63

chosen to diffuse a potentially volatile situation by extending kindness rather than reacting with your Ego. I learned this early on with my willful daughter. Any time I reacted to her obstinacy with force, she met me with more force and we got nowhere. However, whenever I immediately reacted to her orneriness with love, she softened and listened reasonably.

Still, there are many who conceive of Love as weak and therefore, ineffective (spare the rod and spoil the child). Again, this falsehood is fabricated all the time in the media. Look at the tendency of "reality" shows to depict dishonesty and shrewdness as an attribute – *if* it gives an advantage. The message is, "If you are not ruthless, you are weak". In truth, Love is absolute power and can only be dampened when fear disenchants us into believing otherwise.

Judgment rules when we allow our Ego, with its limited view of materialism, to shade our perception and create fear. It seizes control like a despot in a land of servitude. The Ego thrives on fear because it feeds its belief in separation and satisfies its need for self-indulgence.

Tyrannical leaders have always understood this paradigm and employed fear to coerce the masses. How else in history would followers have ignored their true nature and committed heinous crimes against each other? Consider the multitude of precious lives that have been ended when rulers disguised fear with righteousness. "This is the true way, the only way" they have cried as they slaughter those who do not agree. "For the benefit of the whole, we must suppress (or eliminate) those who think or act differently" is the mindset that continues to allow millions to be persecuted.

Judgment that leads to conflict is *always* based in fear.

Part IV

Love...

12

Is Eternal

"In some ways, the rhythm of birth and death is like a breath taken and exhaled...you are not it, yet it comes into you and leaves you, and without its continuous flow you could not physically exist."

- Jane Roberts, *The Nature of Personal Reality*, 1974

Love is eternal and pervasive. Love springs forth as joy and abundance in every variation of form, sound, scent and taste imaginable.

On a particularly glorious autumn day, I experienced Love in an unexpected way. It was while taking my dog for a walk in the neighborhood. As I left my home, I heard the most exquisite music carrying from inside a house across the street. It was my neighbor playing Debussy's *Clair de Lune* on her piano. Her window was open, so the sound was penetrating. The neighborhood, also exceptional in beauty, with flora and wildlife abounding, punctuated my senses with a feeling of immense love. Had I been eating a peach and smelling jasmine, it would probably have been euphoric. Then again, I am easily moved by beauty.

Love, eternally reflected in esthetics is easy to appreciate but, Love displayed intangibly is even more sublime. I am constantly moved to tears by acts of Love; the military personnel and civil servants who willingly endanger themselves on our behalf; an author who has perilously brought reading to the children and women of Pakistan, so they might have access to the rest of the world; the parents in my town of Orlando, who relentlessly sought for their missing daughter – five years after her disappearance; my sister, who exhaustively cared for her husband with Lou Gehrig's Disease, until he took his last breath; the many kind and generous people who have shown tremendous love and support to my family through the years are all demonstrations of love in action.

It is difficult to grasp the magnitude of Love, much less, express it in words. How can our being fathom infinite, eternal Love? It may be possible to glimpse, or even be transported to an awakening through contemplation or meditation. If we took the time to gaze into a clear night sky, open our minds to the realization that the distance never ends, imagine that depth as a white light that radiates in all directions and fills every atom of our being, and steep in the immensity of that vision, we could achieve a sense of the oneness that is Love.

It is equally challenging to explain the endurance of Love. Though, it is like a loving parent who would never banish his child for exerting her free will and *forgetting* she is Love, but would wait patiently for the wayward teen to find her way home to a loving embrace – it never ends.

Love *forever* revives the spirit and restores peace, relationships and health. Have you ever found that after a harsh argument with a beloved, you reflect and realize how much you truly love them and regret hurting their feelings? That is the remembrance of Love. Or else, have you had the chance to feel kindness and compassion toward others or the self after having been diagnosed with a grave illness? That is the voice of Love. When you have been dis-eased, have you ever just given yourself nourishing attention and felt better? That is the intelligence and power of Love.

Most profoundly, Love resides as a unique imprint on our everlasting souls. Long after someone has relinquished the need to experience a physical life and sheds their human vessel, it is comforting to know that their love will be felt and remembered forever. It is said that grief is evidence of Love enduring. Love's expanse has no boundaries.

Love...

13

Releases Fear

"Love is the only freedom in the world because it so elevates the spirit that the laws of humanity and the phenomena of nature do not alter its course."

- Kahlil Gibran, *The Prophet*

Fear offers its own perspective, yet remains a misguided separation from our true self. When in alignment with love, we are connected to our infinite source of vitality and have nothing to fear. When we forget we are connected, conflict and dis-ease occurs.

"No one would have ever placed it [structure] above him had he not forgotten, denied or separated in some manner from the love that he is. Structure has gained seniority simply by default." **-Glenda Green, *Jesus Speaks: Love Without End*, 1999**

Albeit, Fear as a tyrant, can manage only as far as structure will allow, until which point, Love will overcome. When enough destruction has been inflicted and resources have been exhausted to reveal Fear's emptiness, we can gain insight into the endless supply of Love. Like heroes who, without hesitation, would selflessly risk their own life to save another, a true heart of Love expels fear. Love is all you need (The Beatles wrote about this) to erase any perception of separation.

Just as Nature fearlessly perseveres to restore balance and unity, truly *enlightened* revolutionaries have kindled the torch of unity by igniting the unstoppable power of Love. Petrarch understood this, Ghandi employed it and Martin Luther King, Jr. demonstrated it. Even Albert Einstein, whose work with the atom paradoxically led to the deaths of many lives in World War II, was innately aware of oneness:

"A person experiences life as something separated from the rest — a kind of optical delusion of consciousness. Our task must be to free ourselves from this self-imposed prison and, through compassion, find the reality of Oneness."

Albert Einstein

For years now, we have been hearing a mantra for change but, we have been relying on the same old failed methods to try and achieve it. When the approach is exclusionary (if it does not attend to the needs of the whole), it is bound to fail. If there is an underlying agenda, founded in fear to suit the needs of the few, it will not endure.

Fear has eclipsed love for so long that many new and innovative approaches have been immediately shot down before they could even take flight. It will take incredible courage and resolute faith for change to spring forth and soar.

I, for one, am ready for the challenge and there are millions upon millions willing to do the same. Let us collectively set aside our differences and seek a common ground for the sake of humanity. Our false beliefs have paralyzed us for too long.

"You think you are being terrorized by other people, but in truth, you are being terrorized by your beliefs."

-Neale Donald Walsch, *Communion with God,* 2000

At this most opportune moment in history, when mankind is open for change and ideas can be transmitted instantly, I invite you to suspend judgment, relinquish your fears, and be the Love that you are. Join me **FROM FEAR TO ETERNITY, on a path to peace.**

"Because you will not be judged [by God], you cannot be condemned. Because you will never be condemned, you will know at last that Love is unconditional"

-Neale Donald Walsch, *Communion with God*, 2000

"I believe that unarmed truth and unconditional love will have the final word in reality. This is why right, temporarily defeated, is stronger than evil triumphant."

- Martin Luther King, Jr.

Afterward

*"All the darkness in the world
cannot extinguish the flame of a single candle."*

- Saint Francis of Assisi

I wrote this book with the sincere intent of helping to change lives. For many years, I have sat in silence while I witnessed suffering over matters people thought were out of their control. At times, it seemed as though they were creating their own turmoil and most often, the conflicts were over different points of view. Either way, people claimed or portrayed themselves as victims and looked for someone to blame. To me, it made no sense but still, I remained quiet.

I watched incredulously while crowds listened to fear mongers perpetuate lies to advance their own agendas. This did nothing but create conflict. I felt that if people would just heed their hearts and open their minds to a unified vision of the world, that it would shed light on much of the misconception. But, who was I to impose my beliefs without being asked?

As happens, the masses did start to question authority and I felt obliged to share what I have known in my heart and mind – a knowing that instills Peace.

My thought was to present Universal Truths to help remove obstacles and awaken a latent knowing in other souls. I felt that by using the relatable and Universal language of Nature, so as not to provoke earthbound egos, this could be achieved and set forth to do so.

I humbly thank you for being a part of who I AM and being open to my message of PEACE.

Acknowledgments

With great pleasure, I pay homage to the many fellow souls who have inspired and affected my life:

My mother, Carol Terry, who modeled fortitude and instilled in me a love for music and entertaining, as well as gifted me with a robust physique and a talent for creativity; My dad, John Terry, Jr., who showed me resilience, taught me to find joy in dancing and swimming and bestowed on me his aptitude for mechanics; My adored husband, Mark, who is a mirror of my soul; my incredible siblings, Roger, Shannon, Johnna, Jay, Kelly, Tom, Brooke, Cameron, and Courtney, who are the kindest, most loving people I know; John Simon, my grade school science teacher, who inspired me like no other to learn; Curtis Elmore, who, with great patience, helped me discover I was an athlete; My favorite author, Pat Conroy, whose brilliant prose has often brought me to tears. I would also like to acknowledge the multitude of prophets, philosophers, visionaries, writers, artistic performers and brilliant messengers who have illuminated my life with their profound gifts,

Further Exploring

Dr. Joan Borysenko and Herbert Bensen, MD.
Minding the Body, Mending the Mind. Massachusettes: Da
Capo Press, 1987

J. Bronowski. *Science and Human Values.* New York:
Harper and Row, 1956

Deepak Chopra. 40+ Books on Spirituality and
Quantum Physics, 1989-

Dr. Wayne Dyer. Most anything he has written.

Masaru Emoto. *The Healing Power of Water.* California:
Hay House, 2006

Glenda Green. *Love Without End.* AZ: Spiritis, 1999

Esther and Jerry Hicks. All the *Abraham Books.*
California: Hay House, 1997-2010

Napoleon Hill. *Think and Grow Rich: The Original
Version Restored and Revised.* California: Wilshire Books,
1999

Barbara Marx Hubbard. *Birth 2012 and Beyond.* United States: Shift Books. 2012

Michio Kaku. *Einstein's Cosmos.* New York: Atlas Books, 2004

Bruce Lipton. *The Biology of Belief.* CA: Hay House, 2005

Shirley Maclaine, *Out on a Limb.* New York: Bantam Books, 1983

Lynne McTaggart. *The Field.* NewYork: HarperCollins Publishers, 2008

Lynne McTaggart. *The Bond.* New York: Hay House, 2011

Marlo Morgan. *Mutant Messenger Down Under,* New York: Harper 1994

Carolyn Myss. *The Anatomy of the Spirit.* New York: Three Rivers Press, 1996

Carolyn Myss. *Energy Anatomy.* Audiobook. Sounds True, Inc. 2001

Richard Panek. *The Invisible Century,* Viking, 2004

Candace Pert. *Molecules of Emotion.* New York: Touchstone, 1997

Candace Pert. *Everything You Need to Know to Feel Go(o)d.* CA: Hay House, 2006

John Polkinghorne. *Quarks, Chaos & Christianity.* New York: The Crossroad Publishing Company, 1996

Gerald H. Pollack. *Cells, Gels and the Engines of Life.* Washington: Ebner and Sons, 2001

Jane Roberts. *The Eternal Validity of the Soul.* California: Amber-Allen Publishing, 1972

Jane Roberts. *The Nature of Personal Reality.* CA:Amber-Allen Publishing, 1974

Mona Lisa Schultz, MD, PhD. and Dr. Christiane Northrup. *Igniting Intuition.* California: Hay House, 2005

Mona Lisa Schultz, MD, PhD. *Awakening Intuition.* New York: Harmony Books, 1998

Steven S. Sadleir, *The Theory of Existence & The Science of Consciousness* Amazon: The Self Awareness Institute, 2012

Bernie S. Seigle. Anything he has written.

Eckart Tolle, *A New Earth.* New York: Penguin Group, 2006

Eckart Tolle, *The Power of Now.* Canada: New World Library, 1999

Neale Donald Walsch. All of the *Conversations With God* Books. New York: Hampton Road, Putnam and Atria Books, 1996-2021.

What the Bleep Do We Know? Film. Captured Light Industries, 2004

Gary Zukav. *The Dancing Wu Li Masters.* New York: Bantam Books, 1979

Gary Zukav. *The Seat of the Soul.* New York: Simon & Schuster, 1989.

Notes

Notes